BEAUTIFUL BIRDS

WILD & FREE BIRDS
ADVENTURE & COLORING BOOK

KRISTI TRIMMER

AlaskaWildandFree.com
KristiTrimmer.com

It is quite serendipitous to see the photographs I took as I traveled through the U.S. come to life as coloring pages in this book. I'm a huge animal and nature lover and enjoy bringing that wildlife to the pages of my coloring books.

I spent four years solo camping in National Parks throughout the U.S. as a travel writer. Never in my wildest dreams did I think my six-week adventure to Alaska would result in loving this state so much that I moved here. I'm an Alaska artist and writer, and I absolutely love it.

Alaska is my muse, her beauty my playground.

Follow my Alaska and travel adventures at KristiTrimmer.com and find stickers and magnets that match many of these illustrations at AlaskaWildandFree.com.

Thank you to my family and friends for supporting me as I've lived this life that is a little less ordinary, and a little bit more wild and free.

~ Kristi

Table of Contents

Bald Eagle

Barred Owl

Blue Jay

Cardinal

Flamingos

Golden Eagle

Great Blue Heron

Hummingbird in the Desert

Kingfisher

Magpie

Parrot

Peregrine Falcon

Ptarmigan

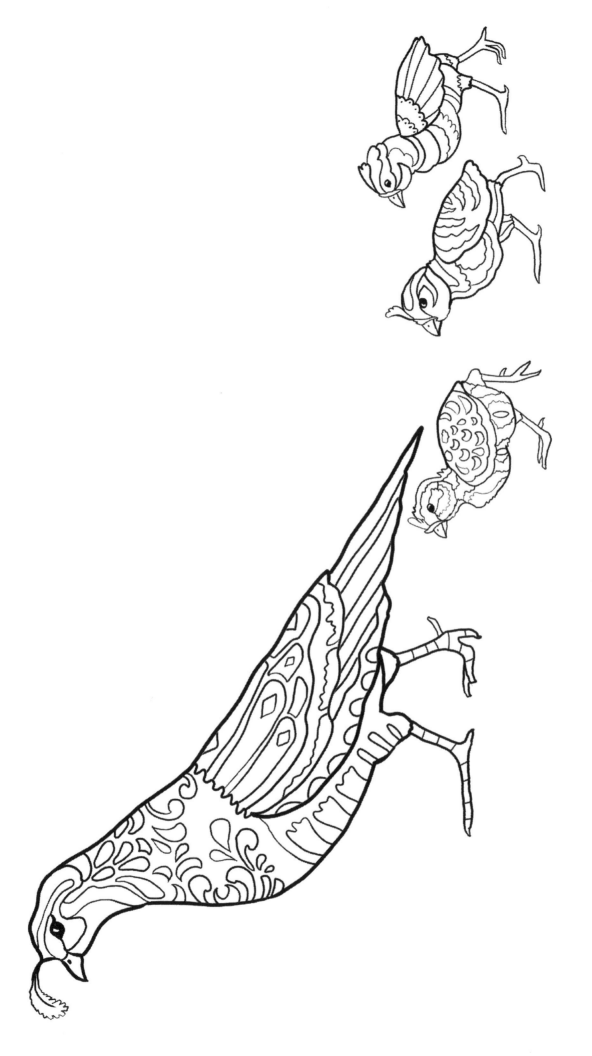

Quail Family

Raven

Red Tail Hawk

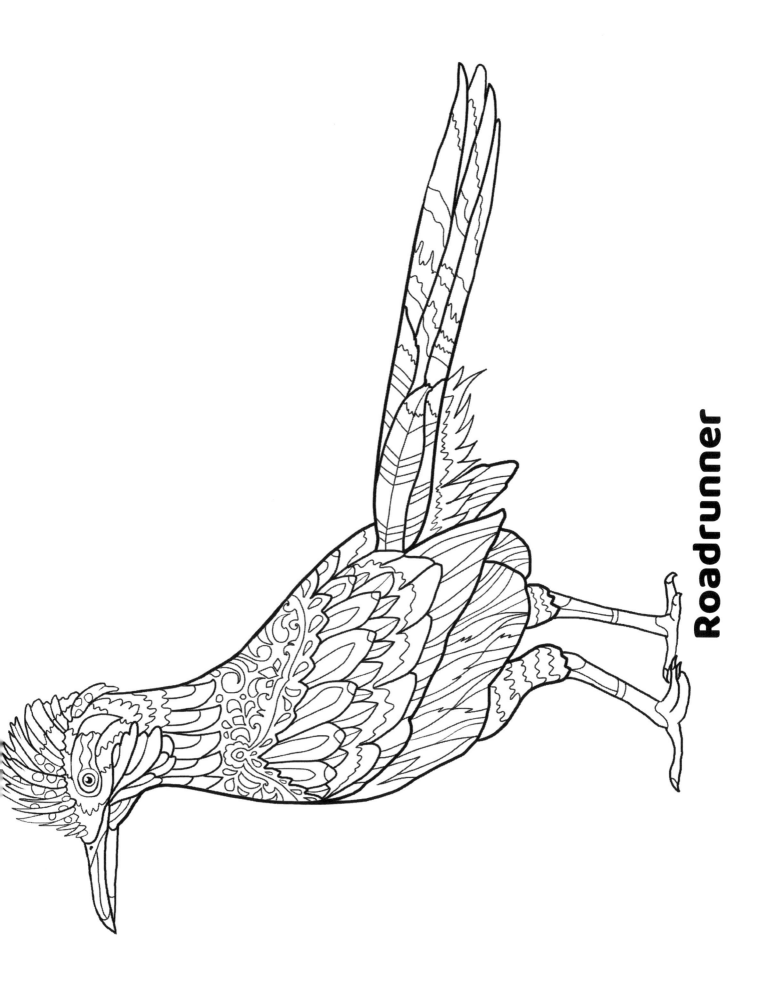

Roadrunner

Thick Billed Murre

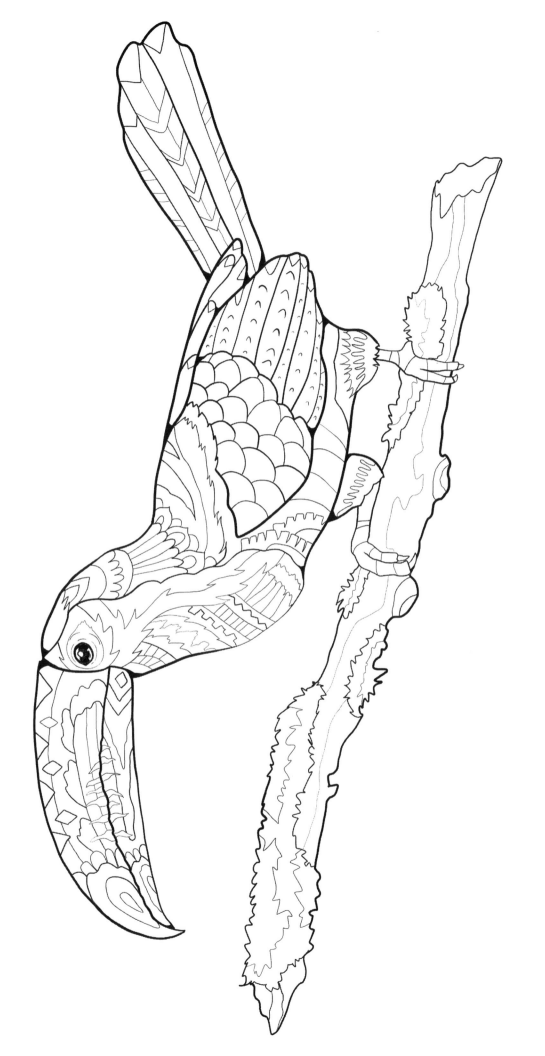

Toucan

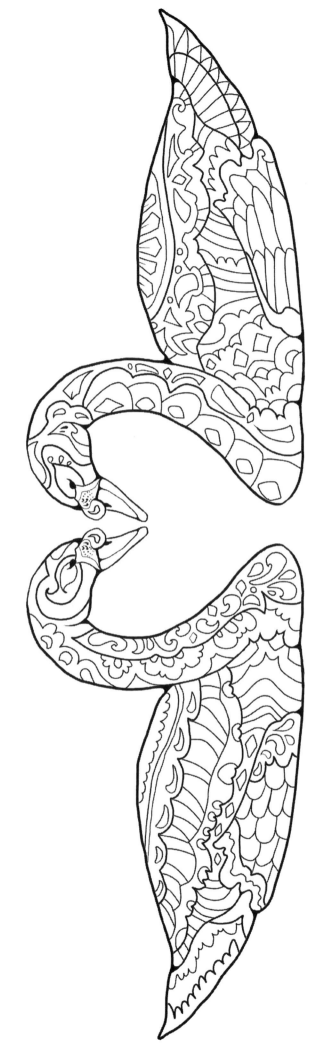

Trumpeter Swans

Tufted & Horned Puffins

Toucan

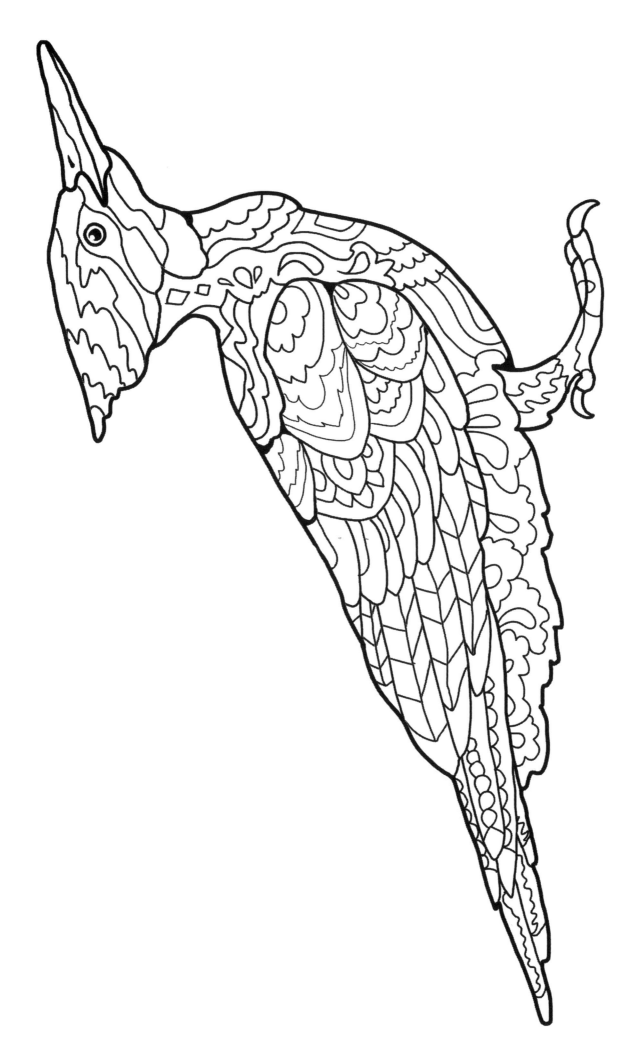

Woodpecker

Wren

Made in the USA
Columbia, SC
13 April 2024

34263790R00030